Potential

Becoming Her. Building Legacy. Blooming in Purpose.

Fatima Anne

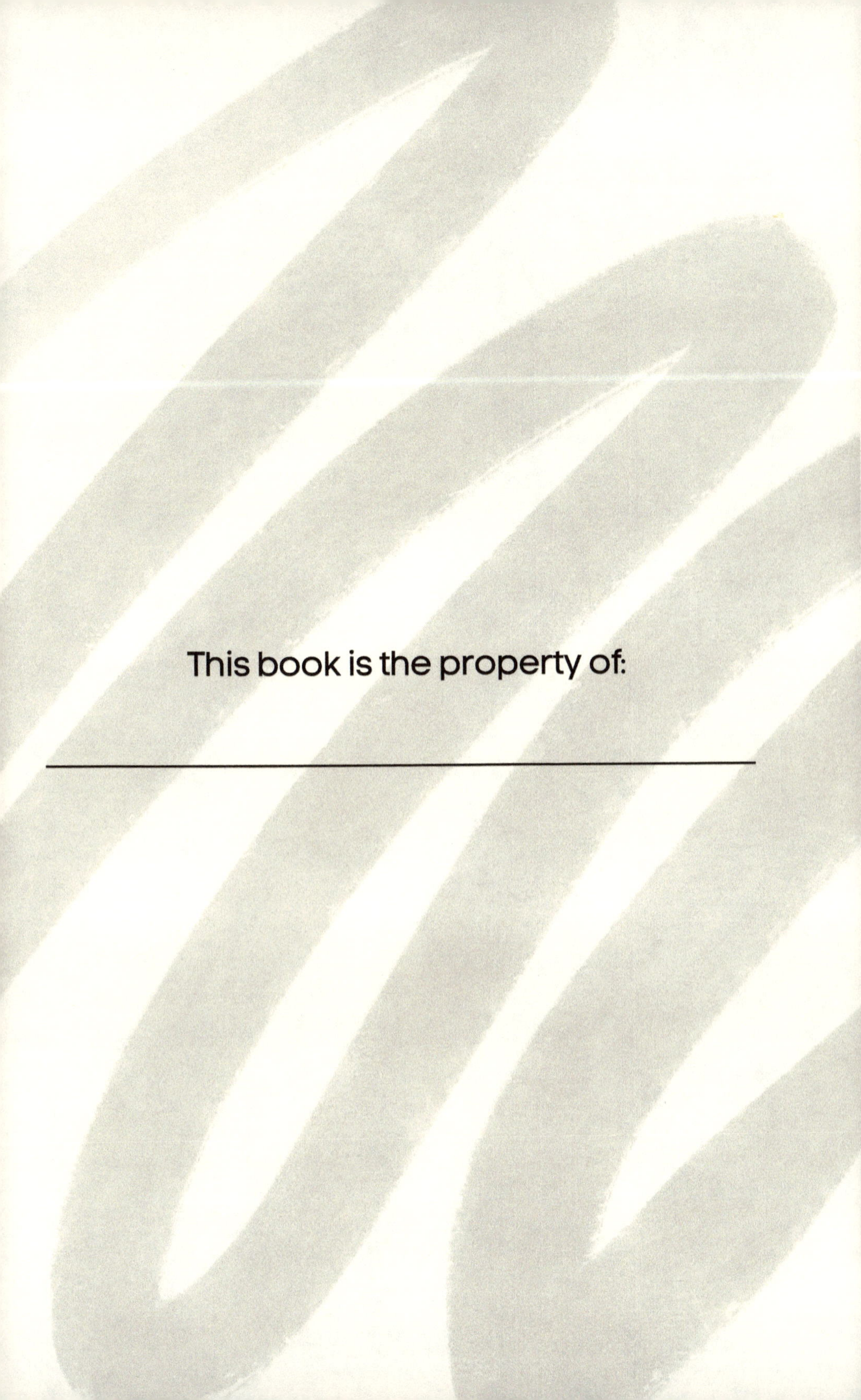

This book is the property of:

Tips for Effective Journaling:

Consistency is Key:

Set a regular journaling schedule to cultivate a habit of self-reflection.
Consistency allows you to track your growth over time.

Date Every Entry:

It's not just about memory; it's about witnessing your evolution. You'll
look back and realize how much you've grown between the lines.

Honesty and Openness:

Be honest with yourself during the reflection process.
Embrace the duality within and use the journal as a safe space for
exploration.

Don't Edit the First Draft of Your Feelings.

You can't heal what you censor. Give yourself permission to be messy
on the page. Growth isn't linear, and neither is journaling.

Reflect, Don't Just Record:

Go beyond what happened to how it made you feel. Ask yourself what
it taught you, what it revealed, what it's preparing you for.

Creativity and Personalization:

Feel free to personalize your journal with doodles, sketches, or
additional notes.
Engage your creative side to enhance the journaling experience.

Tips for Effective Journaling:

Set the Scene:

Light a candle. Pour tea. Grab your favorite pen. Create a ritual around your journaling, make it feel like a date with your higher self.

Pair It with Sound or Silence.

Play the Potential playlist if music unlocks emotion for you, or sit in silence and listen to your heartbeat. Both are gateways to clarity.

Use the Journal Prompts as Invitations, Not Instructions:

If a prompt doesn't resonate, skip it. Or rewrite it. These pages are yours; personal, private, powerful.

Revisit Your Words Often:

Come back to old entries every few weeks. Highlight your breakthroughs. Forgive the parts of you still learning. This is where potential becomes realized.

End Each Session with Gratitude:

Even if all you can say is, "I showed up." That alone is worthy of thanks.

REMEMBER!

Journaling isn't about finding the perfect answers.
It's about discovering that you were the answer all along.

Dedication

For every woman who thought her story ended in the dirt.

This is proof that seeds don't stay buried.

This is for my Babeters, my goddaughter, my nieces, my friends, and every soul who has whispered, "I know there's more for me."

This is for you.

RISE, ROOT, BLOOM.

—Fatima Anne

Preface

When I started writing Potential, I wasn't sitting in a glow and I kept quitting.

I was sitting in the dirt. Bills, heartbreak, doubt, exhaustion. I didn't feel like I had potential at all. I definitely felt like I was under the dirt.

But the more I reflected, the more I realized: buried is not the same as dead. Seeds are buried too. And seeds don't stay seeds. They push. They grow. They bloom.

This book is not about perfection. It's about becoming. About saying yes to yourself when it feels scary. About learning in the dark when you can't see the way forward. About setting boundaries that offend people but protect your bloom. About redefining money, love, and legacy in ways that build beyond survival.

So read these chapters slowly. Pause at the journal prompts. Listen to the playlist. Let the affirmations sink in.

Most of all, let this book remind you that your potential isn't "someday." It's right now, unfolding with every breath you take.

Acknowledgments

First, to God and the Universe: thank you for planting me when I thought I was buried. Thank you for whispering when I couldn't hear myself, and thank you for never letting my light stay dim for too long.

To my ancestors: your resilience is in my blood, your prayers are in my bones, and your sacrifices are the reason I get to stand here and dream out loud. I carry you in every page, every word, every bloom.

To my family: you are both my why and my witness. Thank you for teaching me love, patience, accountability, and laughter. You remind me daily that legacy isn't just built, it's lived.

To my friends and my village: thank you for the late-night talks, the encouragement, the tough love, and the reminders that even when I felt empty, I was never alone.

To every woman holding this book, thank you. Thank you for trusting me with your time, your heart, and your story. This isn't just my book, it's ours. May these words meet you exactly where you are and walk with you into where you're becoming.

And finally, to the woman I used to be: thank you for not giving up. You had no idea how much was waiting for you on the other side.

With love,
Fatima Anne

CHAPTER ONE:

SEEDS DON'T STAY SEEDS

I used to think the dirt meant I was dirty.

There was a time in my life when everything looked still on the outside, but inside, I felt buried. Not planted, buried by bills stacking, life was lifing, and heavy expectations. I was trying to hold it all together while quietly wondering if I was falling apart. I remember thinking, "This can't be all there is for me", but I didn't have proof yet. Just a feeling.

And sometimes, that's all a seed has: pressure, darkness, and a quiet knowing that something is shifting underneath the surface.

The weight of everything; my mistakes, my heartbreak, my silence, the choices I made when I didn't know better, and the ones I made when I did, all felt like proof that I wasn't built for more. The dirt stuck to my name. It showed up in how people looked at me. It stuck to my choices; the relationships I stayed in too long, the opportunities I talked myself out of, the times I played small to keep the peace.

It definitely stuck to my skin. At night, I cried in silence, and in the mornings, I had to get up and still be "mom," still be "strong," still show up like nothing was breaking inside me.

I tried to scrub it off. Tried to outwork it. Tried to outgrow it before I understood it. But here's the thing nobody told me: Seeds only grow in dirt. You can't bloom in the light until you've been buried in the dark. And baby... I've been buried plenty of times.

The Weight of Dirt

There were moments when I thought potential was a pretty word meant for other people. For the ones who had a blueprint, a plan, a daddy with money, or a family who knew what they were doing. But me? I had bills stacking faster than I could breathe. I had to figure things out in real time; with kids watching, with responsibilities that didn't pause just because I was overwhelmed.

I had a mind full of whispers:

You're behind.
You should've known better.
What if this is as far as you go?
And I had a heart that kept loving people who didn't know how to hold it.

It wasn't because I was weak, but I was still learning what I deserved. That was my dirt.

Real dirt looks like:

- choosing survival over alignment because you have to
- staying quiet when you should speak up because you're tired of conflict
- making decisions under pressure instead of in peace
- carrying responsibility for everybody while silently breaking yourself

That kind of dirt doesn't just sit on top of you. It sinks in. And every time I thought I was finished, life dropped me deeper in. There's always another setback, another lesson, and another moment where I had to choose whether I was going to stay there or grow there. I didn't realize it then, but I know it now. I wasn't being buried, I was being planted.

The First Sprout

The first sprout doesn't look like much. It's not a glow-up. It's not a big announcement. It's not a "look at me now" moment. It's a quiet shift. A crack in the ground, a green thread daring to touch the sun. That's how my "yes" began. It was quiet, shaky, unsure, but determined. I kept thinking my ducks need to be in a row, but I didn't need to have it all together. I just needed to push through anyway.

For me, that first yes came the day I realized I was tired of asking for permission. Permission to dream, to rest, to leave, to stay, to shine. I woke up one morning, looked in the mirror, and whispered, "This can't be it."

That whisper turned into a roar.

Lesson One: Stop Apologizing for Dirt

Babe, your dirt is not your disqualification. It's your foundation.

The nights you cried yourself to sleep and still showed up the next day, that's strength. The jobs that drained you dry, that's clarity. the love that left you empty, but forced you to find yourself again. They're all compost. Fuel. Soil. Fertilizer for what you're about to grow.

Don't hide it. Don't clean it up for other people's comfort. Don't let anybody make you feel less because your story started in survival.

Remember: every tree, every flower, every fruit we eat started the same way; buried under the dirt.

Where are you planted right now?

"My beginnings were buried, not broken. I am the dirt and the bloom."

What parts of your life feel like dirt right now?

"My dirt is not my disqualification, it is my foundation."

What dirt am I ashamed of that could actually be my soil?

"The soil remembers what it's meant to grow."

How could that dirt be the very soil where something new grows?

"Growth doesn't ask for permission; it just happens quietly,
then all at once."

Dear Me,

Keep Becoming,

CHAPTER TWO:
LESSONS IN THE DARK

Darkness has a way of stretching time.

Five minutes in the dark can feel like five hours, five months, five years. When you're in it, you forget what light even looks like. You wonder if morning is a myth, if happiness is just a fairy tale told to keep you from giving up. But the dark isn't just where things end. It's also where things begin.

When the Lights Went Out

I used to ask God, "Why me?"

When I was in a season where I couldn't see past the pain. Bills overdue, love gone wrong, kids needing things I didn't know how I'd provide. Nights when the only light in the room was the glow of my phone screen, showing me everybody else's highlight reel while I sat in the shadows of my own life.

Because the truth is there were nights I didn't have answers and just thoughts that wouldn't turn off. Lying there, replaying decisions, second-guessing myself, wondering if I missed something or if I was the problem. The dark got really honest with me. No distractions. No applause. No validation. Just me and my truth. And that's when I realized the dark doesn't lie to you. It reveals you.

But the shift did not happen all at once. I did not wake up one day suddenly strong and clear. It came in small, uncomfortable moments where I had to sit with myself instead of running from what I felt.

First, I had to stop numbing it. No more pretending I was okay just to get through the day. No more distractions just to avoid the truth. I had to actually feel what I had been pushing down.

Then I had to get honest about where I was. Not where I thought I should be. Not where I used to be. Where I was emotionally, mentally, financially, and spiritually. That kind of honesty is uncomfortable, but it is also where clarity begins.

After that, I had to release the blame. Not just blaming other people, but blaming myself for everything that did not go right. I had to understand that everything I went through was not proof that I was broken. It was proof that I was learning. Slowly, my questions started to change.

Instead of asking, "Why is this happening to me?" I started asking, "What is this trying to teach me?"

Instead of asking, "Why am I here?" I started asking, "What do I do from here?"

Because asking why keeps you stuck in the pain. Asking what now puts you back in your power.

What the Dark Teaches You

The dark teaches patience.

Seeds don't grow overnight. Healing doesn't happen overnight. You don't wake up whole just because you said one prayer.

The dark teaches honesty.

You can't hide from yourself when there's no spotlight, no applause, no validation. You either face your reflection or drown in it.

The dark teaches faith.

You learn how to trust that the sun will rise even when you haven't seen proof yet.

Breaking the Silence

I realized I wasn't the only one sitting in the dark. Women all around me were carrying secret storms, smiling in public but breaking in private. That's when I decided to stop pretending.

There's power in saying out loud: "I'm not okay."

Not because it fixes everything immediately, but because it cracks the silence open. And even the smallest crack lets light through.

Lesson Two: Don't Fear the Dark

Babe, your dark season isn't a death sentence. It's preparation.
The dark is where your roots strengthen, where your vision sharpens, where your spirit learns to hear whispers it was too busy to notice in the daylight.

Don't rush through it. Don't curse it. Don't let shame silence you in it.

One day, you'll look back and realize the dark was your greatest teacher.

What did your last dark season teach you? What did you keep hidden in the dark, away from love ones and why?

"I do not fear the dark; I grow in it."

While in the dark what needs to be said or acknowledged so the light can be seen again? Who or what needs to be released because they've become the storm?

"My darkness was never empty, it was a classroom for my becoming."

Who or what did you outgrow while you were healing?

"What broke me didn't bury me, it built roots where light
could find me later."

What would you say to the version of
yourself that survived it?

"Even the moon learned to shine by surviving the night."

Dear Me,

____

Keep Becoming,

____

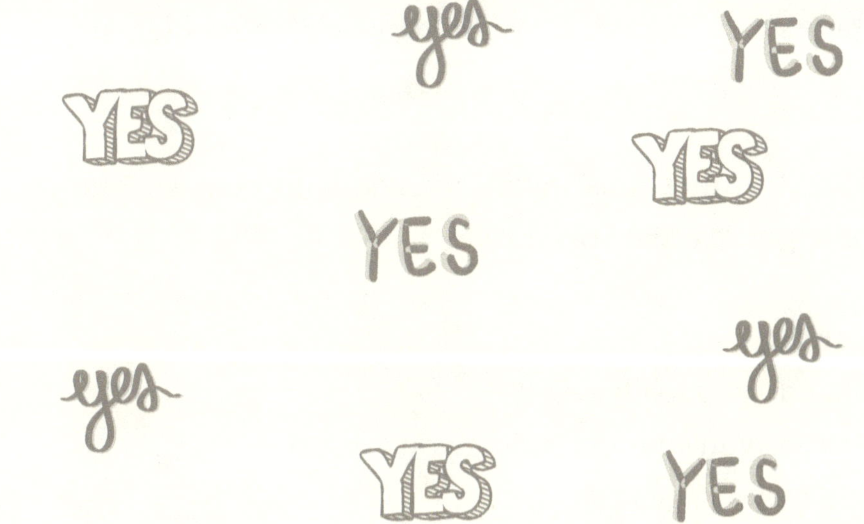

CHAPTER THREE:
THE FIRST YES

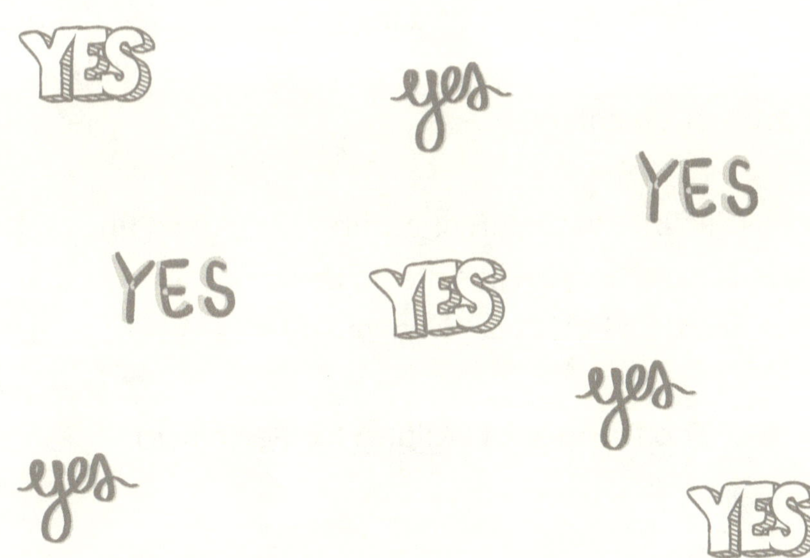

There's a moment in every woman's life where silence feels louder than words.

When the questions you've been dodging echo so loud you can't ignore them anymore:

Who are you?
What do you really want?
Why are you still pretending you don't deserve it?

That's where my "first yes" found me. It wasn't in a church, a boardroom, or on a big stage.

It found me in the quiet, standing at the sink with my hands in dishwater, staring out the window like freedom was right outside the door and I couldn't get to it. Moving through my day, taking care of everything and everyone, but feeling like I was missing myself in the process. I was doing what needed to be done. Showing up. Handling responsibilities. Keeping things together. But deep down, something felt off. Not broken. Just... incomplete.

I had settled into a version of my life that looked fine on the outside but did not feel like me on the inside. And in that quiet, I heard it. Soft. Clear. Unavoidable. Say yes to yourself.

The Danger of Waiting for Permission

I had spent years waiting for somebody else to crown me worthy.

Waiting for a man to see me the way I saw myself in my best moments. Waiting for family to validate my choices. Waiting for friends to clap loud enough for me to believe it. Waiting for life to feel stable enough before I made a move.

I kept thinking, when this lines up, then I will go. When I feel more ready, then I will choose myself. When somebody confirms it, then I will believe it. But the truth is, that moment never comes because some people will never give you that yes. Not because you do not deserve it, but because they are used to a version of you that makes them comfortable, or maybe your growth highlights their stillness. And every time you wait, you stay. Waiting for permission is how potential dies quietly. Not with noise, not with failure, but with delay.

The First Yes Is the Hardest

My first yes was not glamorous. There was no announcement. No big reveal. No neon sign flashed "SHE FINALLY DID IT". No moment where everything suddenly made sense. My first yes came with trembling hands and a cracked voice.

It looked small. It looked like me deciding to write, even

when nobody was reading. It looked like me choosing rest, even when guilt told me I had not done enough to deserve it. It looked like me setting boundaries and feeling the shift in relationships that no longer fit. It looked like me believing in something I could not fully explain yet. It looked like choosing myself in quiet moments that nobody else could see.

And if I am being honest, it was very uncomfortable.

I remember a conversation where I said something simple, but different. I spoke up instead of brushing it off. I did not over-explain. I did not shrink it to make it easier to receive. And the energy changed. Not because I was wrong, but because I was no longer the version of me they were used to. That moment showed me something I could not ignore. Growth will reveal who is aligned with you and who was only comfortable with your silence.

There were moments I questioned it. Moments I almost went back. Moments where the old version of me felt easier. But every time I chose that yes, even in a small way, something in me got stronger. That first yes scared me. But it also saved me.

Yes Is a Muscle

Here's the secret: the more you say yes to yourself, the stronger you get. It's like lifting weights in the gym. At first, it hurts. At first, you doubt you can carry it. But then one rep becomes two, two become ten, and before you know it, you're carrying things your old self would've collapsed under. It is a practice. One decision turns into two. Two turns into consistency. Consistency turns into confidence.

You are speaking up where you used to stay quiet. Walking away from what no longer aligns. Moving forward, even when you do not have full clarity.

That is the power of your yes. Yes is the muscle that builds momentum.

Lesson Three: Your Yes Will Offend Somebody

Not everybody will clap when you choose yourself. Some people will call it selfish. Some will try to guilt you back into silence. Some will try to remind you of who you used to be. Some will swear you've changed. Good. Change is the point.

You are not here to stay the same for the comfort of others. You are here to grow. Your yes isn't meant for everybody's approval. It's meant for your alignment.

And once you understand that, you stop asking for permission. You start moving with intention. And that is when everything begins to change.

Where in your life are you still waiting for permission?
Where have you been telling yourself no for years, and why
don't you believe you deserve a yes?

"My yes is sacred, my no is protection."

What would your first yes to yourself look like if you gave it today? Plan it out so you can give it to yourself.

"The most powerful relationship you will ever have is the one with yourself." — Steve Maraboli

What's one idea I need to say yes to?

The moment you say yes to yourself, the universe rearranges
to meet you there.

If you could whisper one sentence to your future self about
the power of this yes, what would it be?

"The first yes is never loud, it's a whisper that changes everything."

Dear Me,

Keep Becoming,

CHAPTER FOUR:
GLOW IN MOTION

Glow is not a destination. It is not a one-time glow-up, a "look at me now" Instagram post, or a fresh set of nails that fades two weeks later.

Glow is motion. It is always in motion. It is choosing yourself every day, in small ways that compound into something unstoppable.

The Myth of Arrival

For years, I thought glow meant finally arriving. Arriving at the perfect body, the perfect love, the perfect bank account, the perfect moment when everything lined up and stayed that way. But the truth is, there is no finish line. Glowing is not about waiting for that one golden day when everything makes sense. Glowing is the ongoing choice to walk in your worth while the mess is still messy, while things are still uncertain, and while you are still figuring it out.

Identity in Motion

Your glow is how you carry yourself when no one is watching. It is the way you talk to yourself in the morning. It is the boundaries you enforce at work, at home, and in your relationships. The world told me glow was about appearance. Lashes, hair, heels, waistline. Do not get me wrong, I love a good slay. But glow runs deeper than that. Glow is internal. It is the alignment between what you say you want and what you actually do. It is moving in the direction of your higher self, even when your lower self is begging you to stay comfortable.

There were days I did not feel like I was glowing at all. Days I felt tired, stretched, and in between versions of myself. I was still showing up, still figuring things out, still carrying responsibilities that did not slow down just because I needed a moment. But I started noticing something. Even on those days, I was choosing differently. Speaking differently. Thinking differently. That is when I realized my glow was not something I had to wait for. It was already happening.

For a long time, I kept waiting for the moment everything would finally click. I thought once things lined up, then I would feel like myself again. But my glow did not come from perfection. It came from showing up, even when I did not feel like it. Some days my glow looked like discipline. Some days it looked like rest. Some days it looked like choosing myself when it would have been easier not to. That is when I realized my glow is not a look. It is a lifestyle.

Rituals of Radiance

The truth is, discipline is sexy.

There is a different kind of glow that shows up when you start treating your body like home. Drinking water like it is your favorite cocktail. Moving your body because it deserves motion, not punishment. Feeding yourself food that does not just fill you but fuels you. I remember a season where I was pouring into everything and everyone while neglecting myself in the process. I was skipping meals or grabbing whatever was quick. I kept telling myself I would rest later and promising I would get back to me when things slowed down. But things did not slow down. So I had to make a shift. Not a big one, a real one. Choosing to eat better even when I was busy. Choosing to move my body even when I was tired. Choosing to pause, even if it was just for a few minutes, to check in with myself. It did not look perfect. It looked intentional.

Glowing is also spiritual. Your glow grows when you pray, meditate, journal, or sit quietly with yourself. When you declutter your spirit the same way you declutter your closet, you create space for clarity, peace, and alignment. These rituals are not about perfection. They are about momentum. One act of love a day is enough to start the chain reaction.

Lesson Four: Glowing Is Evidence

Babe, your glow is the receipt of your work. It's proof you're tending to yourself, even in hidden places. People may ask what you're doing differently. You don't have to hand them a product list; you can tell them: I'm moving differently. The glow is not what you put on. The glow is what shines out because of what you put in.

What daily rituals make you feel radiant?

"Glow is evidence. My life radiates alignment."

Where do you need to align action with intention so your
glow stays in motion?

"Nothing can dim the light which shines from within."
— Maya Angelou

Where in your life are you still dimming your
glow to make others comfortable?

"My glow isn't for show, it's a prayer I wear."

What does consistency look like when it's
done with love instead of pressure?

"My shine is sacred work, proof that I've turned healing into rhythm."

Dear Me,

____

____

____

____

____

____

____

____

____

____

____

____

____

____

____

Keep Becoming,

____

THE GLOW-UP MAP.
This Year I'm Blooming In...

This Glow Map is not about becoming someone else.
It's about becoming more of who you already are, on purpose.

BODY	MONEY

RELATIONSHIPS	FAITH

LEGACY

You've done the hard part. You've faced the truth, sat in the discomfort, and started choosing yourself in ways you may not have before. Now it's time to move. Not perfectly. Not all at once. But intentionally.

CHAPTER FIVE: LOVE, LOSS, AND LIBERATION

Love will teach you things you didn't sign up to learn.
It will be your sweetest teacher and your harshest critic.

Love will whisper lullabies one night and slam doors the next. And still we chase it, crave it, cradle it, even when it cuts us. Because love, whether it lasts or not, has a way of rearranging the furniture of our souls.

When Love First Glowed

There's nothing like that first spark.

The way it makes you forget your past pain. The way it makes you feel seen in a way you did not even know you needed. For a moment, you believe this is it. This is the love that will finally heal every broken piece of you. Everything feels aligned. Everything feels possible.

I have loved deeply. The kind of love that makes you believe in forever, even when forever starts to feel uncertain. I am not someone who loves halfway. When I love, I am all in. Present. Loyal. Invested. And because of that, I also had to sit with a truth that was hard to accept. Love does not always stay the way it starts.

That realization will stretch you. Because you are not just grieving the person, you are grieving the version of yourself that existed inside that love. The version that felt safe. The version that believed this was where you would land. And when that shifts, it feels like everything shifts with it.

But here is the lesson nobody tells you. Love does not erase wounds. It exposes them. It brings everything to the surface. Every insecurity you thought you buried. Every fear you thought you healed. Every part of you that still needs attention. Love holds up a mirror, and sometimes what you see is not comfortable, but it is honest.

And if we are being real, sometimes we do not just fall in love with a person. We fall in love with what we hope they will fix. We look for people to soothe wounds we have not taken the time to heal ourselves. We look for reassurance to replace insecurity. We look for consistency to calm our chaos. We look for validation to confirm our worth, but love does not save you. It reflects you. It does not fix what is broken. It amplifies what is already there.

If you feel whole, love expands that. If you feel uncertain, love will expose that. If you are still healing, love will bring those wounds to the surface, whether you are ready or not. That is why it can feel so intense. Not because the person is everything, but because the connection is touching parts of you that have been waiting to be seen.

The Weight of Loss

Loss comes in layers.

Sometimes it is loud and undeniable. A breakup. A betrayal. A moment that changes everything. But sometimes loss is quiet. It is a slow shift. A conversation that never gets finished. A distance that grows without explanation.

Loss is not just romantic.

It is friendships that fade when you start growing in a different direction. It is family relationships that feel heavy when you begin setting boundaries. It is people who once chose you daily but slowly stop showing up the same way. It is realizing that not everyone is meant to grow with you, even if they started with you. That kind of loss can be confusing. Because nothing "big" happened. There was no clear ending. Just a quiet understanding that things are no longer what they were.

I have experienced loss that felt like air leaving my body. Walking away felt like suffocation. Nights where the bed felt too big, too empty, like I was drowning in space that used to feel full. And I have also experienced the quieter losses. The friendships that no longer felt aligned. The relationships where I had to choose myself, even when it created distance.

Both kinds of loss change you.

That question will either break you or rebuild you. Because loss, as painful as it is, carries a kind of mercy. It strips away everything that is not real. It forces you to meet yourself without distraction, without attachment, without illusion. And somewhere in that process, something shifts. Not all at once. Not perfectly. But enough for you to see clearly.

The Door Called Liberation

Liberation does not happen the day they leave. It happens the day you stop shrinking yourself for people who do not see your light. It happens the day you stop negotiating your worth to keep something that is no longer aligned. Liberation is a decision.

It is deciding that you deserve to be loved in your fullness. That you do not have to beg to be chosen. That you do not have to make yourself smaller to maintain a connection. It is understood that solitude is not something to fear. It is where you meet yourself again.

Babe, let me tell you something, freedom after heartbreak feels like walking out barefoot into the sun after years in a locked room. You squint, you stumble, but damn, the air tastes different.

Lighter. Clearer. Honest. Losing parts of love taught me something I needed to learn. I can love fully without losing myself in the process. I can show up with an open heart and still have boundaries. I can give without abandoning who I am. That was my liberation.

Love Redefined

Love is not supposed to chain you. Love is not supposed to drain you. Love is not supposed to demand your silence.

Real love liberates. Real love expands you. Real love sees you, respects you, and stands beside you as you grow, even if growth changes things.

Lesson Five: Love Doesn't Complete You

Love doesn't complete you, you are already whole. The right love will remind you of your wholeness, not convince you of your lack. It will not make you feel like you have to earn your place. It will meet you where you are and allow you to be fully seen without shrinking.

Don't confuse intensity with intimacy. Don't confuse possession with devotion. And don't confuse staying with being chosen. Because the truth is, the greatest love you will ever experience is the one that does not require you to lose yourself to keep it.

What love did you lose that taught you the most?

"Love does not complete me, it liberates me."

What version of love are you ready to bury
so a better one can grow?

"Sometimes losing them is how you find you."

What has heartbreak taught you about your own strength?

____

____

____

____

____

____

____

____

____

____

____

____

____

____

____

____

____

"Letting go isn't weakness—it's how wings remember they can fly."

Dear Me,

Keep Becoming,

CHAPTER SIX:
THE POWER OF NO

(and the Magic of Yes)

There's a special kind of freedom in a well-placed "no."

Not the timid no, not the half-hearted no, but the BOLD one.
The one that comes from clarity. The kind of no that feels
uncomfortable at first but settles into your spirit like truth.
The kind that closes doors you were never meant to walk
through in the first place.

For a long time, no was hard for me to say. It felt unnatural.
Like I owed people access to me. My time. My energy. My
presence. Just because I could give it. I thought saying no
would make me difficult. I thought it meant I was letting
people down. I thought it would change how people saw
me.

But I started noticing something.

Every time I said yes to something that did not feel right, I
felt it in my body. Not later. Not after the fact. Right then.
Tension. Irritation. Exhaustion. A quiet resistance that I kept
ignoring because I wanted to be agreeable. Because I wanted
to be seen as dependable. Because I did not want to disrupt
the peace.

But I was disrupting my own.

That was the part I had to face. Every time I said yes to
someone else at the expense of myself, I was betraying my

own needs. My own boundaries. My own alignment. And that kind of self-betrayal adds up over time.

The Weight of Yes

Yes is powerful, but if you hand it out like candy, it loses its sweetness.

Every yes is an agreement. It is a contract with your time, your energy, and your spirit. And once I understood that, I had to slow down and really ask myself what I was agreeing to.

Was I saying yes because I wanted to, or because I felt obligated?
Was I saying yes from alignment, or from guilt?
Was I saying yes out of clarity, or out of fear of disappointing someone?

Because every yes to something that does not feel right is a no to something that does. Saying yes to everybody meant saying no to myself. And that came at a cost. A cost in energy. A cost in peace. A cost in identity.

Self-betrayal is one of the most expensive debts you can carry, because it slowly disconnects you from who you are.

The NO That Saved Me

I remember the first time I said no without explaining, without apologizing, and without trying to make it softer for someone else to receive. It was not dramatic. It was simple. Clear. Direct. And I felt it immediately. My heart raced and my palms sweated, but when the words left my lips, I felt taller. Relief. For the first time, I felt like I had chosen myself without negotiating it.

That no didn't just close a door, it opened space. Space for rest. Space for dreams. Space for the right yes to find me. Space to think clearly. Space to reconnect with what I actually wanted instead of constantly reacting to what others needed from me. And in that space, I started to see how much I had been overextending myself just to be accepted. That was the moment I understood my no was not rejection. It was protection. And once I started honoring that, everything began to shift.

The Magic of Aligned Yes

Here's the secret: once you master your no, your yes becomes sacred.

It becomes intentional. It becomes clear. It becomes something you choose, not something you fall into. When you start removing what does not align, you create room for what does. Your yes is no longer driven by pressure, guilt, or habit. It is driven by awareness. And that kind of yes carries weight. It multiplies. It leads you into opportunities that feel right instead of forced. It connects you with people who respect your boundaries instead of testing them. It builds a life that reflects your values instead of your obligations. A clear no sharpens your yes. And a strong yes moves your life forward.

When you say yes after pruning your life with no's, that yes is charged with power. It's not out of guilt or fear, it's out of clarity.

The right yes, multiplies.

It opens opportunities you couldn't imagine. It aligns you with people who honor your light. It becomes a magnet, pulling your future closer with every step.

Lesson Six: Boundaries Are Bridges

A no isn't rejection, it's redirection.

It is a boundary that leads you back to yourself. It is a decision that protects your energy so you can use it where it actually matters. It is a way of honoring your capacity without shrinking your worth. Boundaries are not walls meant to keep people out. They are structured. They are clarity. They are the bridge between who you have been and who you are becoming.

And when you start honoring those boundaries, something powerful happens. The right people adjust. The wrong ones reveal themselves. And the life that is meant for you starts to meet you differently. Because you are no longer available for everything.

You are available for what aligns.

Where in your life do you need to start saying no?

"When you say yes to others, make sure you are not saying no to yourself." — Paulo Coelho

What is one yes you've been holding back on that deserves
your voice today?

"I release guilt for choosing myself. I am not selfish for surviving well."

What does your peace cost and are you willing to pay it?

"My boundaries are love in structure; they teach others how to treat my peace."

What parts of you are tired of performing peace instead of living it?

"Every no I give is a yes to peace I can keep."

Dear Me,

Keep Becoming,

CHAPTER SEVEN:

MONEY AIN'T JUST MONEY

Money isn't just paper.

It isn't just numbers on a screen or plastic cards in your wallet. It's energy. It's access. It's an opportunity. It's the difference between surviving and building, between borrowing and owning, between working for a dream and funding one.

And the truth? For a long time, I had a love-hate relationship with money. I loved what it could do, but I hated how it made me feel. I hated chasing it. I hated stressing over it. I hated how it could shift my mood, my decisions, and sometimes even my confidence. There were seasons where I felt like no matter how hard I worked, it never stretched far enough. Bills came fast. Responsibilities came faster. And I was doing what so many women do, holding everything together on the outside while quietly trying to figure it out on the inside.

The Lies We Inherited

Most of us were taught money in whispers and warnings.

"Don't ask for too much."
"Money doesn't grow on trees."
"Be grateful for what you get."

Nobody sat me down and explained credit, assets, investments, or ownership. Nobody explained how money moves, how it grows, or how it can be used as a tool to create freedom. What I inherited was fear. Fear of spending wrong. Fear of not having enough. Fear that even if I did get money, I would not know how to keep it.

But money is not emotional. It is not personal. It is a tool. And tools do not have morals. A hammer can build a house or break a window. It depends on whose hand it is in. That realization changed how I started looking at everything. Money was not the problem. My relationship with it was.

Survival vs. Strategy

There is a difference between surviving and strategizing. When you are in survival mode, money feels like sand slipping through your fingers. You are reacting instead of planning. Paying what is due. Stretching what you have. Hoping nothing unexpected happens. Living one step behind your own life. I know that feeling. I have lived in that space where every decision felt urgent and every dollar already had a place to go before it even arrived.

But survival mode is not a permanent address. At some point, something in you has to shift. Not overnight. Not perfectly. But intentionally. I had to start thinking differently.

- Learning to budget not from lack but from vision.

- Fixing your credit so banks stop seeing you as a risk and start seeing you as leverage.

- Saving, not just for rainy days, but for legacy days (the ones your children will live in when you're gone).

And that is when money started to feel different. Not easy, but clearer. Not overwhelming, but structured. Because I was no longer just reacting to money. I was starting to direct it.

Legacy Money

Money ain't just about paying bills. It's about building bridges.

It is about creating something that outlives you. It is about making sure the people connected to you have options you did not have to figure out on your own. Businesses, property, savings, knowledge. All of it matters.

There was a moment where that became real for me. Not just something I talked about, but something I felt. I started thinking about my family, not just in the present, but in the future. What would they have access to because of me?

What would they struggle with if I did nothing different? What information would they be missing if I did not learn it first?

That is where the Legacy Binder was born.

It did not start as something polished. It started as a need. A need to organize what I was learning. A need to make sure my family was not left guessing. A need to create structure around things that were never explained to me. Accounts, documents, plans, and information that usually gets scattered or ignored until it is too late.

The first time I put my family's name on that binder, something shifted in me. It stopped being just about getting by. It became about building forward. About making sure that what I learn does not stop with me. That my children and the generations after them do not have to start from zero.

I am still learning. Still adjusting. Still figuring things out in real time. But now I move with intention. I ask different questions. I make different decisions. Because I understand that money is not just about what I can do today. It is about what I am setting up for tomorrow.

Lesson Seven: Money Mirrors Mindset

Money reflects how you think. If you see it as temporary, it will move through your hands quickly. If you see it as something to manage with clarity, it begins to stay. If you see it as a seed, it begins to grow.

Money listens to the energy you carry. If you chase it with fear, it runs. If you attract it with clarity, it stays.

Babe, potential without a plan is just a wish. And money without direction will disappear just as fast as it comes.

Money is not just what you earn. It is what you build. It is what you keep. It is what you pass on. And once you understand that, you stop seeing money as something stressful. You start seeing it as something powerful.

What money story did you inherit that no longer serves you?

"Money is a tool in my hands, not a chain on my spirit."

What's one shift you can make today to treat money
like a tool, not a threat?

"Wealth is the ability to fully experience life."
— Henry David Thoreau

What money patterns am I ready to rewrite?

"Wealth starts in the mind, but legacy starts in the heart."

If your money could talk, what would it say about how you treat it?

"Abundance answers when worthiness walks into the room first."

Dear Me,

____

____

____

____

____

____

____

____

____

____

____

____

____

____

Keep Becoming,

____

CHAPTER EIGHT: BUILDING BEYOND YOU

At some point, the glow isn't just about you anymore.

Yes, you start with yourself. Your healing. Your boundaries. Your yes. Your growth. But eventually, the work does not stay contained. It spills over. It touches your children, your partner, your circle, and your community. That is when you realize your becoming was never just for you.

There was a moment where that shift became real for me. A moment where I stopped thinking only about what I needed and started thinking about what I was leaving behind. Not just money, but structure. Knowledge. Options. I started thinking about my kids and what they would inherit, not just physically, but mentally. The habits they would see. The decisions they would model. The way they would understand life, money, love, and themselves because of what I showed them. And I knew in that moment I wanted to give them more than survival. I wanted to give them a foundation. That is when building became bigger than me.

The Ripple Effect

Every choice you make is a ripple, whether you realize it or not. The way you think, the way you move, the way you respond to challenges, all of it travels beyond you.

When you choose to break a cycle, your children inherit new patterns. When you choose to build something for yourself, you show the people around you what is possible.

When you decide to learn, to grow, to take ownership of your life, it gives others permission to do the same. People are watching you who may never say a word. People learn from how you carry yourself, how you handle pressure, how you recover, how you keep going. Your glow is not just lighting your path. It is lighting paths you may never walk yourself. Someone, somewhere, will step through a door you cracked open simply by choosing to become more.

The Family You Build, the Legacy You Leave

Legacy is not just about blood. It is about what you build through love, intention, and structure. It is about what you pass down that cannot be taken away. It is teaching your children how to manage money instead of just spending it. It is modeling what healthy love looks like instead of repeating what you saw. It is creating systems so your family does not have to start over every generation.

For a long time, I was focused on today. Paying bills. Handling responsibilities. Making sure everything stayed afloat. But something shifted when I started thinking about tomorrow. Not just my tomorrow, but theirs. That is when the idea of the estate binder came to life.

It was not about being perfect. It was about being prepared. It was about organizing what I was learning and making sure it did not get lost. Documents. Plans. Information. Things

most families never talk about it until it is too late.
But this was different. This was me deciding that we would move differently. That we would not leave confusion behind. That we would not leave our future up to chance.

That binder was more than paperwork. It was an intention. It was structured. It was proof that I was thinking beyond the moment I was in.

Building Community Wealth

Building beyond you does not stop at your household. It expands into your community. Into the spaces you occupy. Into the people your life touches. How can your growth serve more than just you? How can your knowledge open doors for someone else? How can your voice create access where there used to be limitations?

We are not meant to hold everything for ourselves. We are meant to allow what we build to flow outward. Because real wealth is not just what you keep. It is what continues.
It is the opportunities you create. The conversations you start. The doors you help open. The examples you set.
We are not reservoirs meant to store everything. We are rivers. And when we allow what we build to flow, it nourishes more than just our own lives.

Lesson Eight: Self-Growth Becomes Legacy When It Outlives You

You cannot take the money, the clothes, or the accolades with you. None of it follows you when you leave, only what you built in people, what you poured into others, and what truly remains.

Building beyond you does not mean carrying the weight of the world. It means designing your life in a way that your impact continues even when you are no longer present.
It means being intentional about what you leave behind. Not just things, but systems. Not just memories, but direction. Not just love, but structure. Because the real goal is not just to live well. It is to leave well.

What's one cycle you're breaking so the next generation
doesn't have to fight the same battle?

"I build not just for me, but for generations after me."

What blueprint do you want your children, family, or community to inherit from you?

"Someone is sitting in the shade today because someone planted a tree a long time ago." — Warren Buffett

What do you want to leave behind besides money?

"Legacy is a language, I speak it through everything I create."

Who are you building for and what do you want them to remember about you?

"The most powerful inheritance I can give is healed lineage."

Dear Me,

____

____

____

____

____

____

____

____

____

____

____

____

____

____

____

Keep Becoming,

____

CHAPTER NINE: POTENTIAL REALIZED

You watered yourself with discipline. You fed yourself with boundaries. You protected your energy with no's. You aligned yourself with yes's that mattered. You chose growth even when it was uncomfortable, even when it was quiet, even when no one was watching. That is what created the bloom.

The bloom is not luck. BLOOM = labor + love + faith.

Living in Alignment

Potential realized looks different than most people expect. It is not loud. It is not perfect. It is not constant highs and flawless moments.

- Waking up in peace instead of panic.

- Loving yourself enough to walk away from what drains you.

- Seeing money as leverage, instead of something to fear.

- Building a legacy that stretches further than your own timeline.

Alignment is not perfection. It is consistency. It is choosing to live in rhythm with your higher self, even when life feels uncertain. It is making decisions that reflect who you are becoming, not who you used to be.

I used to think becoming meant arriving somewhere. Like one day I would feel finished, complete, settled in a way that never shifted. But now I look at my life and see something different. I am already living things I once prayed for. And I am still growing. Still stretching. Still evolving. That is the beauty of it. I did not miss my moment. I became her.

The Mirror Moment

Stand in front of your mirror and look at her. Not quickly. Not critically. Really look.

That woman staring back at you is the proof. Proof that seeds sprout. Proof that darkness teaches. Proof that yes builds and no protects. Proof that love does not break you, it reveals you. Proof that you made it through seasons you thought would take you out.

You are not who you used to be. And that is not something to mourn. That is something to honor. Because potential realized is not about becoming someone else.
It is about finally becoming yourself.

Lesson Nine: The Work Never Stops, But Neither Does the Bloom

This is not the end. There is no final version of you that stops growing. You will keep planting. You will keep pruning. You will keep evolving in ways you cannot even

Every scar. Every setback. Every sacrifice. Every moment you thought you were falling behind. It was all part of the blueprint that brought you here.

Potential is not about who you might be one day. It is about recognizing that you already are.

This is not the end. You'll keep planting, keep pruning, keep glowing in motion. But now you know: nothing was wasted.

Every scar, every setback, every sacrifice was part of the blueprint.

Potential isn't about who you might be one day. Potential is about realizing that you already are.

If you were already living as your fullest self today, what would be different?

"I am both the seed and the bloom. Potential is realized in me."

What's one bold action you can take this week to step into that version of you?

"I am no longer waiting to become. I am living proof that the seed was enough." — Caramel Xpressions

What parts of your life today are answers to prayers you once whispered?

"The woman I prayed to become is now praying through me."

How will you honor the woman you've become without
losing sight of the woman you're still becoming?

Becoming isn't about becoming someone new, it's about remembering who you were before the world forgot."

Dear Me,

____

____

____

____

____

____

____

____

____

____

____

____

____

____

Keep Becoming,

____

"My Blooming Season Manifesto"

Since your life is a garden and you are responsible for tending your own soil, what needs to be planted and what weeds need to be pulled?

____

____

____

____

____

____

____

____

____

____

____

____

____

____

What I'm Building Beyond Me

- Who do I want to impact?
- What traditions do I want to start?
- What lessons do I want to pass down?

Dear Me,

Keep Becoming,

A LOVE LETTER
To my Readers

To the woman holding this book,

I need you to know: you are not unfinished.

You are unfolding.

Every day you wake up is another chance to become more.

Stop waiting for permission.

Stop apologizing for your dirt.

Stop doubting your glow.

You are potential realized, in real time.

And the world is waiting for your bloom.

With love,

Fatima Anne

The Glow-Up Map (Appendix)

Think of this as a "living framework" .

Step One: Seed (Awareness)

Identify your dirt (your pain, your patterns, your past).

Step Two: Dark (Growth)

Create one practice that roots you (journaling, prayer, therapy, meditation).

Step Three: Yes (Momentum)

Commit to one small yes to yourself this week.

Step Four: Glow (Embodiment)

Choose 2 daily rituals that align your body and spirit.

Step Five: Legacy (Expansion)

Start a family binder, savings goal, or project that builds beyond you.

Step Six: Bloom (Alignment)

Live your potential daily; revisit this map every 90 days.

The Soundtrack of Potential

Curated by Caramel Xpressions Presents

This playlist is more than background music; it's the heartbeat of becoming. It's the sound of growth, glow, and grace in motion. Every track was chosen to mirror the chapters of your journey, from the buried beginnings to the radiant bloom.

You'll hear the ache of transformation, the softness of healing, the rhythm of resilience, and the anthem of self-return.

It's for the mornings when you need to remember your power, and the nights when you're relearning your peace.

Press play when you're journaling, driving, crying, dancing, or simply becoming.

www.ingramcontent.com/pod-product-compliance
Lightning Source LLC
Chambersburg PA
CBHW022057050726
47591CB00002B/580